don't call us punk because we hate that

ADAM OYSTER-SANDS

POEMS

stb

STEEL TOE BOOKS

est. 2003

don't call us punk
because we hate that

Under the spreading chestnut tree
I sold you and you sold me
There lie they and here lie we
Under the spreading chestnut tree

—George Orwell

TRACK LIST

We don't have to fix everything at once
time don't mean that much to me
don't call us punk because we hate that
That's Just Life (In the Big City)
The summer David worked at both Taco Bell and KFC
Poetry in Motion (The Art of the Dance)
A Dream About Teeth
family reunion
1919
They built a fire station where the church used to be
One semester Jeremy slept on our dorm floor
Most days I'm ready to believe this is all there is
A Child Like Fear
a trueish story from my dad
They Told Us There Were Dead Bodies in Mountain Creek Lake
The one about my short-lived career as the Lazer Trax sign guy
The Last Party in My Hometown
All the kids from the scene have kids now
Truth, What Truth (for Scott)
The Known is Ended (for Jeff)
A stick sharpened at both ends (for Josh)
The Whole World Hates You (for Jesus)
a sound (for the irredeemable ones)
pick up your bags (for Adam)

We don't have to fix everything at once

And these are the things that happened in the time before this one. In the time when Waffle House still had an all-you-can-eat menu, we sat in a booth and smoked the cigarettes we bought from the vending machine in the entry and ate hash browns with our burgers for as long as our stomachs could consume. We were young and desperate to be something you can't hold, something like freedom. The clothes we inherited from older brothers swallowed our bodies like the early winter fog over downtown and we never wondered why we felt so alone. Tim said we had a place to go but it never really felt like home so we asked for more syrup and refills of Coke, never worrying where the time went as it shuffled along to a rhythm just beyond our reach.

And these are the things that happened in the time before this one. A time when we tried to craft our stories out of the songs we blasted through blown car speakers while skating in vacant parking lots to drown the all-consuming din of the suburban sprawl our parents planted for us.

And these are the things that happened in the time before this one. For this is what we created, these stories we tell ourselves in our aging about a time before this one when the world was larger and our growing disillusionment sat just behind our ribs, consuming.

And these are the things that happened in the time before this one. More myth than memory, told through the haze of time and cigarettes and the remnants of all-you-can-eat waffles.

time don't mean that much to me

Sam Cooke said we'll stay here 'til it soothes our souls, even if it takes all night. cause sometimes that's what it takes to keep the darkness at bay, to see the sunrise. and i don't drink like i used to. these days i'm only drunk on nostalgia and the thoughts that maybe i had it figured out at 18 and spent the next decade denying myself. and i don't recognize that town where we spent those spring nights just driving around, aimless in our corner of suburbia. and the park bench by the lake where we pledged ourselves to the present is still there, but we are gone. no future was our mantra, so we weren't prepared for the passage of years we never thought we'd see. we weren't supposed to live this long. cigarettes and backroads and music on the car stereo—we thought those were the good times.

another poem about a moment
that never existed. about a mixture
of memory and myth
and what could have been
if we had been honest with ourselves.

and i don't want to go   back

i don't want to go   back

i swear i don't want to go   b a c k

so i'll stay here all night long.
time don't mean that much to me.

don't call us punk because we hate that

once we played a show
in a record store
with a band named after
a porn star.
their singer repeatedly declared
he was more punk
than the rest of us
fuckers.
at the end of their set
he proved it
by macing himself
in the face,
collapsing on the floor
in a ball of mucus and tears and screams.
his band stepped over
his writhing body
to join the rest of us
outside smoking cigarettes
in the crisp december air.

That's Just Life (In the Big City)

Every week we scoured the back
pages of the Observer, before the
ads for sex work disguised as
personals, to find the show flyers.

We missed our exit but still made it in time
to wander the streets and bathe in the neon
glow of tattoo parlors and bars barred to us
and our fake ids which would get us into the show
but no farther. We ate slices of grease dripping pizza
and dodged potholes and the unhoused on the side-
walks while trying to look hard and hide our smiles
as the sun sank behind the growing silhouette of downtown.

     There was so much more to consume
     than we imagined.

We were waking up
to a life we'd only known
in lyrics and music videos.
We'd never felt so far from home.
We'd never been so alive.

ADAM OYSTER-SANDS

The summer David worked at both Taco Bell and KFC meant that our lunch and dinner was covered most days when the heat was too much for sixteen-year-old boys with limited funds and too much time on their hands since I only worked at night keeping score for the city's adult softball leagues where the thick winds blew warm off the lake and stuck to everything and everyone sitting under the bright stadium lights and swarms of summer mosquitoes. I had a car and enough pocket money for the gas necessary to get to a free meal as I aimlessly drove the winding streets, with the windows down and the stereo up loud thinking that those lazy summer days would last forever like the songs we wrote and played in my garage on out of tune instruments.

> And the holy spirit
> followed us around
> after David's mom
> Norma sang hymns
> in her kitchen while
> we loaded his drums
> into the back of a car
> strewn with Taco Bell
> wrappers and KFC
> buckets left from
> too many days
> and too little
> responsibility.

Our shirtless bodies stuck to the red cracked vinyl seats of my Chevy in the suffocating heat as the tape deck played our teenage anthems through blown speakers and we thought we'd never stop sweating the grease from our daily meals through the pores of our skin hoping that maybe this would be the summer where our fortunes would change like the ones in the movies we watched on those rare nights we were off work together because we thought if a guy like Lloyd Dobler could get a girl like Diane Court then there was some kind of hope in the universe for guys like us who were haunted by the moral reckoning of an invisible man in the clouds and our mothers' loveless nights with husbands barely more than just physically present and those were the things we tried to write in our songs but the heat was so heavy in the garage we almost passed out from dehydration and a boredom we recognized as privilege as we drove from one fast food restaurant to the next wishing this would last forever and yet hoping for something better over the horizon which shimmered in waves through the windshield of my car during that summer when we were just sixteen and felt alive. And we never wanted that season to end like a drag from the last cigarette you will ever smoke where you inhale so slow because you know when the ash hits the filter this decade long relationship that has been simultaneously life sustaining and life consuming is over with nothing left to show but the little wisps of smoke above your head and the tar in your lungs and the comforting knowledge that the two of you will meet once again when the time is right and necessary.

Poetry in Motion (The Art of the Dance)

Strongarm Chris worked at the skate shop
in the mall and sold us trucks and bearings
and talked about the virtues of metalcore.

Straightedge Davey gave me a copy of
The Jungle and a Facedown Records
comp so I could learn the rules of the scene.

Strongarm Chris grabbing Straightedge Davey
from behind and running around the pit like
he was wearing a Baby Björn as the band
on stage spun guitars around their back before
everyone lost their shit on the breakdown

was fucking poetry in motion.

A Dream About Teeth

I swallow a tooth in a dream
where you pull them from my
mouth one at a time. This isn't
a malicious act, but one of love

and restitution. The next tooth you
pull bounces on the scratched hard-
wood floor of my bedroom and
rolls under the couch that once lived
in my grandmother's sewing room.
My thoughts dwell on people I once
knew but left behind under the guise

of growing up. And you pull another tooth
as I sit on the floor, mouth open, staring at
the popcorn ceiling in my living room and
I think about those jokes I once told that
pushed you away while I tried to hold you

close. And my mouth is numb and full
of blood but I keep smiling as you grab
another tooth and pull like tabs on the
bottom of a flyer in our college dorm
advertising an open room in a three bed-
room apartment just across the lake near
the warehouse where we recorded those
songs when we were moving in opposite
directions but pretending to still be on the
same page. We traveled thousands of miles

together then stopped. Another tooth you
pull from my mouth slides across the bath-
room tile and the blood is starting to
concern me when I catch a glimpse of

my bruised and swollen face in the mirror.
I'd like to wake up now, but instead I
see the drum set we found tucked in the
back of a storage closet in the church
where our parents sang together in the
choir and plotted for us to be more.

I think I only have a few teeth left and
wonder if anyone's invented time travel
because there are some things I need to
fix but the clock keeps turning the wrong
way and another six months have passed
and I'm still sitting under the dining room
table I inherited from my mother. I worry
the blood from my mouth will stain the
antique wood like the blood from your fore-
head stained your t-shirt when you tripped
into the cymbals trying to maneuver around

the unkempt cables on stage. And we laughed
so much back then, as if we would be seventeen
forever. But then I grew rigid and slowly sank
into the floor where I was trapped for so long.
And I understand why you had to go,
but understanding doesn't mean healing.

I realize this night is long overdue.
Because when she didn't wake up
from her nap, I wasn't there for you.

And it's far too late for apologies. So
I swallow the last of my teeth in a
dream and it feels right and righteous.

In the end,
I suspect we become what we abide.

family reunion

i once took my sister
to a blink-182 show
in a club,
before they were
the soundtrack
for jocks
and frat parties,
before they played
amphitheaters and MTV.

they sold thongs
along with t-shirts and cds.
from the stage,
tom gave a detailed
description with visuals
about the proper way
to perform a blowjob.
my sister
was 14.

twenty years later
she and i sang dammit
together
at a karaoke bar
and laughed.

1919

We lay on a blanket in the backyard near the gap in the fence
that James made for reasons unknown and watch the stars slowly
appear while our neighbors are harassed by the cops who patrol
our street inventing reasons to stop their car.

And we hear Rick yell because he knows the last bastion of DIY
in our town is nearing its end—between the law and the internet
he can't keep it going as the kids grow up and find other avenues
for expression beyond Saturday night sing-alongs and Sunday
afternoon potlucks.

But when our upstairs toilet broke
and we couldn't afford to fix it
we knew we could go next door
and have our needs met
with dignity and single ply paper.

They built a fire station where the church used to be

I heard a symphony about a vanishing city.
But we all could write that poem these days.
None of our homes can remain intact amidst
the economic value of eternal exponential expansion.

And even if your town somehow held guard against the very nature
of time itself, then your eyes aren't the same as when you rode your
bike to the park on the first morning of summer. You had some really
good times there but you can't tap back into the innocence you felt
when the world was huge and just down the street from your house.

And tonight we drive the same solitary streets
and can barely recognize the concrete
and red bricks in the sidewalks on Main.

And I wonder if anyone in this sleepy suburb is thinking of me
the way I'm thinking of them all these years after I crossed the
state line, leaving everything behind like Beth did when she went
to Yale and was raped her freshman year but still didn't come
home cause Yale is a real ticket out and up and beyond our reach.

ADAM OYSTER-SANDS

And I hope she made it
cause we lost touch after everything collapsed.

The way this place fucks you up.
The things this place demands of you.
That's not a symphony I need to hear.

And this is another type of nostalgia we don't need.
Cause the calendar's current carries our cares away
and back again like a metronome slightly off beat.

I know this story's not unique.
In the end no one learns the lesson.

What does that say about us?

One semester Jeremy slept on our dorm room floor

Jeremy had a van and lived in the country.
Our band played a graduation party in his backyard
and I spent the whole-time sneaking cigarettes with Dana
and vaguely paying attention to this kid from the sticks.

I didn't know then that he would show up
at our dorm a few months later with a trash bag
full of clothes and guitar equipment
and a notebook full of songs.

He slept on an egg crate on our floor
and challenged Jeff in Dr. Mario tournaments
while we went to class. We could sneak him
food from the cafeteria and never thought
about the trouble we were causing.

He had a van to haul our shit around
and needed a place to sleep. So over winter break
he came home with me and stayed at my mom's house
to avoid the frigid weather when the dorms closed.

Jeremy left abruptly one morning after my mom asked
him to take a shower because she was concerned with
the conditions of the bed sheets in the guest room.

I felt bad about him sleeping in his van but the request
seemed reasonable. We all do what we have to keep
our punk cred I guess. Like how I started washing my
hair only once a week and with a bar of Irish Spring
instead of shampoo because that's what Jeff and John 5-0
did and I thought their hair looked fucking rad.

And when Jeremy finally started his band
I was jealous. They were sick as hell
even if they mostly ripped us off.

Most days I'm ready to believe this is all there is

How do you get the truth back
when you left it at the bottom of an empty whiskey bottle
by the train tracks where we tagged Tolstoy's face
on an abandoned boxcar using the stencil James made
before he moved to a farm outside Eugene / Even now
when the right song plays I am transported back to that moment /
And the diesel fumes from the distribution center near the tracks
fills my nostrils across thousands of days / And I can feel
the burning in my throat as I swallow sip after sip
of cheap bourbon / Each drink a feeble attempt to move past the past
and an identity defined by an invisible truth demanded and dreaded /
Each swallow a chance to forget the people and places
and performances perfectly crafted for devotion / Each ounce
of liquid fire a preparation for what is to come after all I know
has ended / So it goes / And so my friends say behind my back
as they paint my name on a wall / A reminder of apostasy and to pray
for my soul / The fear of a god hangs heavy in the distance between us /
A bourbon brown baptismal / I fashioned the truth into a new life /
Most days I'm ready to believe this is all there is

At a New Year's Eve party in a warehouse I was given chocolate
mescaline by the son of prominent brewers who caused a girl
I knew to almost drive off the road when he stripped down
to a flea market thong in her front seat / And I hit a possum with my car
as I drove home too inebriated to be behind the wheel but too
far lost in my loneliness to care / Across town my friends were praying
the new year into existence without me / So I sat on a curb and cried
in the dark over the life I took and the people I lost while fireworks
exploded in celebration above my head / I mourned my damnation alone /
The taste of poison still fresh on my tongue / This is My blood poured
out for the forgiveness of sins / This is My body broken for you /
So it goes / And I don't remember getting home that night but the next
day I stumbled back to where the possum lay to find only an empty
asphalt road between homes / I found myself on the curb again /
Head throbbing from the choices I made and the too bright new year's sun /
Too dehydrated from the chemicals in my body to find the tears this time /
No angels flanked the road to declare a resurrection miracle this time /
And I can't seem to fashion the truth into anything sustainable this time /
Most days I'm ready to believe this is all there is

A SIDE
ADAM OYSTER-SANDS

How do you get the truth back /
The temptation to fall into belief is strong these days

A Child Like Fear

I don't remember much about the time
Vern moved into Exploding House and slept
most nights next to the broken drum set
in the corner of what once was a living room.

As long as the rent was paid on time, the
slum lord who owned the house didn't care
about the almost nightly barrage of house shows
nor the small mountain of cigarette butts
and beer bottles collecting on the back porch.

Condensation dripped from the ceiling on those
unbearably hot summer nights as bodies pressed
and swayed together while some white belt band
screamed about unrequited love and we pushed
the swoops of hair from our eyes like sand.

In a haze of cigarette smoke and the buzz
of too many Lonestars, I saw Dylan play guitar
and sing songs about vampires and Jesus while
using wooden rods duct taped to his shoes to play
keyboard sounds over Lindsay's droning beats.

Dylan painted in my living room for a while before we lost
him to church and the bald charlatan's promise of glory.

I   don't   remember   much.

I do remember the songs
and the feeling that eternity brings.

a trueish story from my dad

if you ever have the chance to speak
with my dad / it won't take long
for him to mention the time he met
stevie nicks at a theater in dallas in 1982
where he was working on the lights
and she was set to perform later that
evening / the way he can weave a story
that's questionably true at best is like
watching birds fly / and i don't know if i do
anything as naturally as my dad spins tales /

guess that's another thing he didn't pass
down / but at least we talk a few times
a year now / unlike the decade plus we spoke
only at forced christmas gatherings / or like
the summer he moved to north carolina and
asked me to drive out with him / two days
in a car / hardly a word worth any weight
transgressed the space between the driver's
and passenger's seat / music played on the
stereo while i just stared out the window
of an american made car, watching towering
old oak trees blur past in a wave like the swifts
spiraling above the school's chimney every fall /

i've spent the last few years learning how
to talk to the man i'm terrified of becoming
but i still can't listen to fleetwood mac

They Told Us There Were Dead Bodies
in Mountain Creek Lake

You were there for it all,
standing in the back, our
unacknowledged fifth member.

Scott and I joked around
as we drove his bug
to pick you up after you

said you were in a car accident
on Mountain Creek Parkway.
Our laughter stopped when we saw

all four wheels of your graduation
present in the air and the woman
from TD Jakes' church told us

that she saw angels lay your car
upside down in that ditch as an act
of mercy. And years later I heard

real suffering for the first time when
the doctor told us there was nothing
more they could do for your mom—

the cocaine was just
too much.

The one about my short-lived career
as the Lazer Trax sign guy

Spin the sign
Twirl around
Walk the median
Turn up the volume
Burn in the sun
Sweat through the shirt
Wave at the cars
Drop the sign
Stumble around
Change the cd
Try not to pass out
Repeat
Repeat
Repeat
Repeat
Repeat
Repeat

Six straight hours in the sun at minimum wage meant a couple of new albums for an afternoon's work waving the record store sign for the Saturday consumers creeping down Cooper. Shrub said he'd pay me in CDs but never said I could take a break.

The Last Party in My Hometown

Paul's parents were in Europe
so everyone eventually passed out
in the various nooks and crannies
of his gaudy suburban mansion
on an unremarkable spring night.

Before that I watched various kids tackle
a golf bag full of clubs at least ten times
in a row after doing an unknown number
of whippets. I showed up a little late
because we played a show earlier

at a church, but when I walked in
after being dropped off, Martin handed
me a Budweiser and Colin laughed at my
Op Ivy shirt while someone played
Putting Shame in Your Game in the

background. I wandered through the haze
trying to recognize the faces of the kids
who never spoke to me in high school,
wondering how I got there. I sat by the
pool with Kirsten and listened to her talk

to some guy I didn't know while mostly
naked people did flips off the diving board.
I smoked cigarettes with Kara's sister Gina
as she gave me a ride home at 7am because
I had to play in the praise band that morning,

still drunk and possibly smelling like shit.
As I hung my cigarette out the passenger
window and watched the familiar roads fade
into each other like brushstrokes on canvas,
I knew that was the last party in my hometown.

ADAM OYSTER-SANDS

All the kids from the scene have kids now
or they didn't make it to their 30th birthday.

What else should I expect when
no future was our mantra?

And there are adults out there
with regrettable tattoos fashioned
after the drawing Scott made
as the cover of our first cd which
also adorns my own arm well into
a decade of life I never expected to see.

We wrote songs about the books
we loved and gave away copies
at the various merch tables in back
of clubs and churches where we spent
our weekends trying to build something.

When we needed money to record
the kids showed up to the benefit show
where Scott put his foot through
a monitor and we ended up giving
most of our take back to the club.

But it didn't matter.

The barrier between the stage
and the crowd dissolved
in a mist of
sweat
and spit
and shared
microphones.

The record came out anyway—
for the kids in the scene
who loved our shitty band
and sang along every weekend.

Most of those kids have kids now
and I hope they get a chance
to lift each other up
and build something
like we once did
back when we were
kids in the scene.

Truth, What Truth (for Scott)

You had a tri-hawk and a copy of The Catcher in the Rye
when we met.

Over a quarter of a century later and you're still here, sitting
outside this bar drinking non-alcoholic beer with me because
we've both been through some shit and come out the other side,
broken but better.

The Known is Ended (for Jeff)

You filled my spot
for a little while
after Brett kicked me
out of the band I started.

I resented you
for a time
but never blamed you.

Once we started playing
together, I saw why
the change was made
and I knew I couldn't hang.

So I worked hard
to make myself necessary
in other areas.

I never understood
why you played with us
when you could
have had so much more.

It's taken time but
I've come to see
that's what friends do.

A stick sharpened at both ends (for Josh)

I've written so many of these poems for you and there are way too many unsent messages clogging the back end of my drafts folder that thinking about it now makes me feel sick like the time I stole earrings from Disney World and met up with our youth group and tried to play it cool until the cop grabbed my arm.

I keep what I can of you.

We came from the same shit town. Sundays full of church and Saturdays full of everything else. I think often about the time we talked your neighbor into playing his bagpipes for us in the street as the afternoon sun barely cracked the treetops. I was shaken by the volume and how we did everything we could to not laugh before we climbed into your Geo Metro and sped off towards CD Warehouse or Taco Bueno.

I keep what I can of you.

I remember when your parents were worried about you so they sent you to that Christian school I almost went to after crying every day in sixth grade. When you returned to high school, we saw each other and never looked back, at least for a while. You were becoming you and I couldn't find the space for it. I was still trying to deny myself for an eternal reward. That isn't an excuse.

I keep what I can of you.

One night the DAT tape messed up so you had to come back to the studio and record your drum parts again. And I laid on the floor and listened to you pound it out on a floor tom and crash cymbal in one take after screaming a joke at my expense. You no longer believed but you kept playing.

I keep what I can of you.

The Whole World Hates You (for Jesus)

At the center of it all was a man called Jesus.
All the songs and the shows and the relationships came
back to the fact that we were raised to see ourselves as lost.
So many years spent in service to a Lord who demanded
our everything like the ever-expanding summer fires
encroaching on our places of solace and safety. Suburbia
set the stage for a duality impossible to reconcile and drove
us into the far-reaching realms of hypocrisy and devotion
played out in every Saturday circle pit and Sunday church pew.

In the end,
We are our only saviors.

In the end,
You can't love this way forever.

In the end,
Something had to give.

In the end,
We were never lost.

a sound (for the irredeemable ones)

ryan didn't shower and he was the most punk kid I knew. nick looked just like kurt cobain, down to the track marks. jeff had liberty spikes and wore safety pins in his face. i couldn't compete with that. my privilege afforded me the chance to explore, to discover, a sound that united us. suburban youth / record shop junkies / food not bombs / duct-taped shoes / summer pool parties and skate sessions / shitty songs / late nights flyer making at kinkos / scotch tape and scissors / labeling and packing the 7-inches we made / the pinnacle of pride / d.i.y.

but all the sweaty sing-alongs and after show ihop hangs couldn't save us from the things we take to numb the desperation in our chests. then josh disappeared after they laid kelly to rest because how do you look at her children, lost in an ever-thickening fog with no sense of up or down, left or right, just breathing. a sound could only take us so far—the place we found had shattered. maybe it was just noise after all.

an ending.

but i remember being fourteen and hearing a sound in colin's bedroom for the first time and not knowing what it was but knowing that all i wanted was to hold onto it and never let go. a sound i didn't know i needed until it revealed itself to me like the subtle acceptance of a lover who pulls you out of an unnoticed monastic state. a sound that perfectly captured my teenage awkwardness and loneliness and frustration at the blasé nature of my stubbornly mediocre suburban existence. i had a skateboard and hand-me-down jeans and the trap of middle-class expectations. they had mohawks and leather jackets and something that seemed like freedom. in that moment, a path was revealed like emerging from a dark wood into the brilliant warmth of the summer sun, a jarring momentary blindness, then, clarity of sight and a way through.

a beginning.

A SIDE   ADAM OYSTER-SANDS

pick up your bags (for Adam)
i grew up
in a tradition
that forbade
dancing.
there was
something impure
about the way
our bodies move
they said.
the flesh
after all
is carnal—
the vessel
of sin and
damnation
they said.
and i remember
the fear
i felt
standing
on the edge
of a circle of rage
for the first time.
and i remember
the music,
the movement,
the human heat,
the dance.
and i remember
the hands
that picked me up
and protected me
when i fell.
is this memory

or myth?
these stories we
tell ourselves
about a moment
of time
in a life
that extends long
beyond its
expected close.
this is not
my story
but the story
of a million
suburban kids
bored and broken
and looking
for something
that can't be held,
for something
like freedom.
and i don't want
to go back.
and i don't want
to be the person
i was back
when i yelled
in a dark club
trying to reach
out a hand to
the local kids
sweating it out
to the songs
we wrote
in jeff's living
room. that

was our dance.
and it meant
nothing
and it meant
everything.

twenty years
after our
final show
the movement
has changed
and yet
i am here,
still dancing.

ABOUT ADAM OYSTER-SANDS

Adam Oyster-Sands is a high school Language Arts teacher and poet. After writing cringey song lyrics in his younger years, he began writing poetry with his students as a practice on craft and voice and an expression of identity. Since then, Adam has had a number of poems published in various literary journals and magazines such as Picture Frame Press, Indolent Books and Allegory Ridge as well as winning an award from the Oregon Poetry Association. Though his back may revolt, Adam still enjoys trying to land a kickflip, the occasional circle pit, and fucking shit up before 10pm. He can often be found hiking up mountains and running through forests with his partner Morgan and their puppies near their home in Portland, Oregon. don't call us punk because we hate that is his first chapbook.

ACKNOWLEDGEMENTS

"don't call us punk because we hate that" was originally published in *Verseweavers*: the Oregon Poetry Association Anthology of Prize-winning Poems. Number 24/2019 by The Oregon Poetry Association, 2020.

ADAM OYSTER-SANDS

www.ingramcontent.com/pod-product-compliance
Lightning Source LLC
LaVergne TN
LVHW041205080426
835511LV00006B/743